BRA

ANDREW HUBERMAN

THOUGHTS AND INSIGHTS

FROM THE

NEUROSCIENTIST, PROFESSOR AND PODCASTER

-

CREATED BY:
BRAIN PICKING ICONS

Brain Picking Andrew Huberman: Thoughts And Insights From The Neuroscientist, Professor And Podcaster
By Brain Picking Icons

Author: Brain Picking Icons
Contact: contact@brainpickingicons.com

INDEX

ABOUT ANDREW HUBERMAN

Andrew D. Huberman, an American neuroscientist and associate professor in the Department of Neurobiology at Stanford University School of Medicine, was born on September 26, 1975, in Palo Alto, California. He has made contributions to the fields of brain development, brain plasticity, and neural regeneration and repair. His research on the visual system, particularly the mechanisms governing the activation of the brain's circadian and autonomic arousal centers by light, as well as the control of conscious vision or sight by the brain, receives a lot of attention.

The phrase "Non-Sleep Deep Rest" (NSDR), which Huberman is credited with inventing, describes techniques that induce brief periods of shallow sleep in the brain and body in order to promote neuroplasticity and lessen mental and physical exhaustion.

In 2013 Huberman received the McKnight Foundation Neuroscience Scholar Award and a Pew Charitable Trusts Biomedical Scholar Award. For his contributions to the field of vision science and work to restore the visual system and treat blindness, he was given the 2017 ARVO Cogan Award.

In addition to serving on the editorial boards of Current Biology, The Journal of Neuroscience, The Journal of Comparative Neurology, Current Opinion in Neurobiology, Cell Reports, and Neural Development, Huberman is an elected member of the National Institutes of Health Grants Advisory Panel on "Neurobiology of Visual Processes." He belongs to the Faculty of 1000.

Huberman launched the "Huberman Lab Podcast" in January 2021, with an emphasis on neuroscience and technologies with a scientific foundation. In it, Huberman speaks with scientists David Spiegel, Alia Crum, Lex Fridman, Samer Hattar, Matthew Walker, Karl Deisseroth, and Robert Sapolsky.

DIET

WHAT HAPPENS TO YOUR MICROBIOTA WHILE FASTING?

Huberman says that during periods of fasting, especially prolonged periods of fasting, we actually begin to digest a large portion of our digestive tract. If the whole thing doesn't start to disappear and there's thinning of the mucosal lining, or at least disruption of the mucosal lining, a lot of the microbiota species can start to die off.

Discovering this was surprising to Huberman, but nonetheless, it's interesting that fasting may actually cause a disruption to certain healthy elements of the gut microbiome. But again, there's a caveat. The caveat is that when people eat after a period of fasting, there may be a compensatory proliferation, meaning an increase in healthy gut microbiota.

WHAT HAPPENS WHEN YOU FAST?

When you are in a fasted state, typically you are going to use fuels that are available to the neurons based on your intake of food the day before. Maybe you'll be using some glycogen, maybe you'll be using some fat. Maybe you'll be using some blood sugar that's derived from other storage sites in the body. However, you don't actually use fat as a fuel source for neurons under typical conditions.

Proteins and fats, glycogen, etcetera, are converted into fuel that neurons can use. What's interesting about this is that when well fed, meaning when blood glucose and sugar are at a properly elevated level in the bloodstream, it can be delivered to the brain in a way that allows neurons to work best.

Your nervous system is extremely metabolically demanding and it loves glucose. Neurons love glucose.

HOW EATING TOO MUCH SUGAR CAN AFFECT HOW YOU PURSUE YOUR LIFE GOALS?

Huberman believes there's nothing inherently bad about sugar. The word sugar gets a bad reputation nowadays, and indeed, you're going to hear over and over again that consuming a lot of refined sugars, in particular high fructose corn syrup, is known to have a very large number of bad effects on the brain and body.

There's nobody that really debates that anymore. Sugar impacts the way that the brain works, such that we tend to seek out more of particular nutrients. For instance, if we eat sugar, there are two, or at least two mechanisms by which we will crave more sugar.

When we ingest sugar, it has a bunch of different effects on the way that our neural circuits work that can allow us to be more or less focused, more or less agitated, more or less happy, more or less depressed.

In some cases, if you're ingesting too much at the wrong times or in the wrong forms, sugar can actually impede those goals. In fact, sugar can prevent all the right behaviors from allowing you to achieve the goals that you want.

PSYCHOLOGY

WHY REWARD EFFORT INSTEAD OF LOOKING FOR EXTERNAL REWARDS?

In a study, researchers observed kids that really liked to draw. They started giving them little gold stars on their drawings -that's an extrinsic reward. Then, they stopped doing that, and the kids stopped drawing. They associated the good feeling of doing it with the external rewards.

Huberman says this teaches us that we have to be very cautious about how much of our internal dopamine we attach to external rewards. If we want to continue to grow and pursue our focus, we have to work hard with a growth mindset, which is the academic and laboratory discovery of Huberman's colleague, Carol Dweck at Stanford.

The hallmark of a growth mindset is really two things. One is, "I'm not where I want to be now, but I will be. I'm capable of getting there." Eventually, the other is to attach a sense of reward to the effort process itself.

In fact, don't reward the resolve; reward the effort. If you look at true high performers, people that are consistently good at what they do, they don't peak and go through the most postpartum depression; they crash and come back. And their life is a cycle of ups and downs, but people who are on that upward trajectory consistently attach dopamine to the effort process.

WHAT SIMPLE TOOLS CAN GET YOU OUT OF DEPRESSION?

If someone is depressed, what they need to do, according to Huberman, is get up early and get some light in their eyes, as well as some movement.

These are not even tips -they're really tools. And they're very powerful because they're grounded in excellent science.

You get that dopamine release early in the day. That's an antidepressant that actually helps you sleep better the next night. Getting sun in their eyes and movement early in the day is, for most people, accessible, so they should absolutely be doing it. Everyone should be doing it.

WHY IS OUR MOTIVATION SYSTEM GENERIC?

The beauty of the dopamine system, just like the stress system, is that it is generic. The fear system is also generic. This means they are designed for a bunch of different scenarios. The motivation system is also generic; it can be used to achieve the next lamppost as the milestone, or it can be used for five miles as the next milestone. You get to control it, so it's completely arbitrary and internal.

If you finish a marathon in first place, no one comes along and drips dopamine in your ear. You self-generate that. It's all about your internal representation. Now, that doesn't mean that there aren't good and bad events in life.

But the fact of the matter is that if you set the next milestone as just outside the distance of what you're comfortable with and you make it there, if you allow yourself a moment to register that win, you get energy to then set the next milestone and achieve it.

That energy is dopamine converted into epinephrine - adrenaline.

There are a lot of people nowadays who take pre-workout energy drinks. They'll drink canned energy drinks or they'll drink a pre-workout and they'll try and get that same big stimulation because dopamine has a stimulant effect. However, there is no epinephrine, a family of molecules that work together to keep you motivated.

Then they'll also exercise to try and get even more of a dopaminergic experience out of that workout. Sometimes it's also to perform. That approach, rather than trying to get your dopamine as high as you possibly can in order to get the most out of an experience, turns out to not be the best approach.

What you'll find is that layering together multiple things, substances, and activities that lead to big increases in dopamine can actually create pretty severe issues with motivation right after those experiences, and even a couple days later.

HOW DOES MOTIVATION VARY DURING THE DAY?

Pretty much everybody follows a schedule of zero to nine hours of motivation after waking. That is, from the time you wake up until about nine hours later, the neuromodulators dopamine and epinephrine tend to be at their highest levels that they will be at any point in the 24 hour period, or in any period of the day.

We can call this zero to nine-hour period phase one of the day. Just for simplicity, from nine to about 16 hours is what we will call phase two. And that's when dopamine and epinephrine levels tend to subside a bit compared to the earlier part of the day, so serotonin levels start to increase.

Then there's phase three of the 24-hour cycle, which is from about 17 hours after waking until about 24 hours after waking, and it's roughly around zero. During that time, there is chaos in terms of which neuromodulators are most present in the brain. What this means is that, during sleep, you have incredible peaks in choline and acetylcholine; you have incredible peaks in dopamine and drops in dopamine; you have incredible peaks in serotonin and drops in serotonin.

WHY WATCHING PORNOGRAPHY CAN MAKE YOUR SEX LIFE LESS SATISFYING?

There are a lot of young guys in particular who are approaching Huberman because they're watching a lot of really intense pornography. There are studies now being conducted at Stanford and elsewhere that show that pornography causes a strong dopamine rush. These are very primitive pathways that, in some ways, can overwhelm the dopamine system.

So a lot of young guys are getting all this arousal from watching other people have sex, and then they're in the real world scenario and they're no longer the third person in it. They're actually in the scene with someone else, and it completely collapses their experience.

If you understand dopamine, it all makes perfect sense. They're getting this enormous dopamine release from something that is external to them, but real life may not mimic the intensity of the combination of variables.

CAN STRESS GROW YOU?

There's a general idea that stress grows you, or that challenge grows you. Huberman thinks this is a very powerful mindset. He surveyed a bunch of different people with different professions and asked, "What's your view of stress? Do you think it grows you, or does it diminish your ability?"

The only group that said, "Stress grows you; the more challenged, the better we get. The more stress you experience, the more likely you are to succeed," was a group from the SEAL teams. Huberman doesn't know if they were new recruits or if they'd been in the Navy for a long time. This is how Huberman learned that if you adopt a mindset that stress grows, you're going to be much better off.

HOW DOES OUR RELATIONSHIPS WITH OUR PARENTS SHAPE OUR ROMANTIC RELATIONSHIPS?

People's orientation toward attachment is defined by their relationships with their parents. For instance, if the parent leaves, the child can get a little distraught, but then can distract itself. Then there are the so-called insecure attachment styles.

According to Huberman, here's what's fascinating: those same neural circuits that create attachment with our parents are repurposed for romantic attachment in adult life.

Imagine a young girl with a secure attachment to her father, and an insecure attachment to her mother. In early adulthood, she will transfer the insecure attachment style to the mother in male relationships, but have great relationships with female friends.

THE BRAIN

WHY IS DOPAMINE VITAL FOR MOTIVATION?

According to Huberman, dopamine has everything to do with how you feel right now, as you're reading this. It has everything to do with how you will feel an hour from now. It has everything to do with your level of motivation, your level of desire, and your willingness to push through effort.

If ever you've interacted with somebody who just doesn't seem to have any drive, or if you've interacted with somebody who seems to have endless drive and energy, what you are looking at there in those two circumstances is without question a difference in the level of dopamine circulating in their systems.

There will be other factors too, but the level of dopamine is the primary determinant of how motivated we are, how excited we are, how outward-facing we are, and how willing we are to lean into life and pursue things.

WHY DO PEOPLE WITH ADHD USE MORE CANNABIS?

One thing that Huberman has found somewhat surprising is that many people with ADHD use or abuse cannabis. You might think, "Well, why would they do that?" ADHD used to think that an increase in dopamine actually led to heightened levels of attention, which is what these people and children crave.

Well, it turns out that cannabis also increases dopamine transmission in the brain, but because of the other chemicals it increases, namely serotonin and some components of the cannabinoid and opioid system, it also creates that kind of alert but mellow awareness.

In other words, THC increases dopamine and other neurochemicals that can also create a state of calm; it's that sort of middle ground.

ADDICTIONS

WHY ARE DRUGS SO ADDICTIVE?

There are many ways to increase your dopamine levels.

Chocolate will increase your baseline level of dopamine. Both the pursuit of sex and the act of sex increase dopamine two times. Nicotine in particular, which is smoked in cigarettes, increases dopamine two and a half times above baseline. However, this peak that goes up above the baseline two and a half times is very short-lived.

Cocaine will increase the level of dopamine in the bloodstream two and a half times above baseline, while amphetamine, another drug that increases dopamine, will increase the amount of dopamine in the bloodstream 10 times above baseline, a tremendous increase in dopamine.

WHY IS SUGARY FOOD ADDICTIVE?

What Huberman thinks is really interesting is that, for hundreds of years, people have thought that food can be addictive because of how sweet foods taste. That would seem to make sense: you eat something that tastes sweet, so you want more of it.

However, it turns out that it's much more interesting than that. When you eat something sweet in your stomach, you activate cells called neurons, which sense the presence of sugary foods, independent of their taste, and signals to the brain.

Acting like sensors, those neurons send information up to your brain. It goes through a series of stations, and then you release dopamine. This molecule makes you want more of whatever it is that you just ingested.

In fact, this pathway is so powerful that they've done experiments where they completely numb all the tastes and feelings in somebody's mouth. They're also blindfolded, so they don't know what they're eating. They are given food that is either sugary or not sugary. What researchers found is that even though people can't taste the sugary food, they crave more of the food that contains sugar because of the sensors in their gut.

MIND AND BIOHACKS

WHAT CAN YOU DO IF YOU FEEL SLEEPY AT WORK?

If you are feeling tired, Huberman says it can actually be beneficial to the wakefulness systems of the brain to look up toward the ceiling. You don't want your chin all the way back, but you want to look up and to raise your eyes toward the ceiling. Look up and try and hold that for 10 to 15 seconds.

This isn't like looking up and closing your eyes on a nice sunny day -that's relaxing. This exercise isn’t about relaxation; looking up at the ceiling actually triggers some of the areas of the brain that are involved in wakefulness. So if you're somebody who falls asleep at work, this can be very beneficial indeed.

WHY PRACTICING A LITTLE SELF-DENIAL IS GOOD FOR YOU?

Huberman does this many times throughout the day: he actively refrains from doing something that he impulsively wants to do. It could be looking at his phone, but it could even be something trivial, like wanting to walk to the kitchen and get a glass of water.

This way, he's actively engaging in self-denial. Why would he do something like that?

Restricting his behavior in some way keeps his dopamine circuits tuned up. Also, not looking at his phone first thing in the morning for an hour is a great habit in itself, because the second phase of sleep and REM sleep, being more predominant in the second wave of sleep, het affected by our phone use.

HOW TO ACHIEVE CONSISTENCY FOR TRAINING?

If you want to start exercising, the important thing is to just get started and get consistent. Even if someone just walks five days a week, it's the consistency that pays off. Huberman thinks it pays off for a different reason than we think.

Sometimes we want to see the physical or financial results right away. But he thinks a big part of it is that you're training your nervous system. Everyone has these things called central pattern generators. These are neurons that are in our spinal cord and brain stem that generate repetitive movements. And the brain loves to load central pattern generators with work because then the mind can think about other things.

A lot of the challenge of studying or taking on a fitness program is because it requires so much deliberate brain activity. If you just decide, “I'm going to do it regularly,” that's a non-negotiable part. Then a lot of that gets handed over to central pattern generators, and it frees up a lot of thinking space.

HOW CAN YOU IMPROVE YOUR VISION?

How can you improve your vision? How can you get better at seeing things? One way is to make sure that you spend at least 10 minutes a day total seeing things off in the distance -that would be well over half a mile or more.

Try and see a horizon, try and get your vision out to a location that's beyond the four walls of your house or apartment. For every 30 minutes of focused work, you probably want to look up every once in a while and just try and relax your face and eye muscles, including your jaw muscles, because all these things are closely linked in the brain stem and allow your eyes to go into a so-called "panoramic vision," where you're just not really focusing on anything. Then you can refocus on your work.

Many people are experiencing severe vision problems because they're not getting enough sunlight during the day. They have sleep problems because they're not observing sunlight early in the day. Also , artificial light stimulation of the eye in the middle of the night affects our vision.

HOW TO INCORPORATE A NEW HABIT INTO YOUR ROUTINE?

If you are deciding to adopt a new habit, Huberman says you just have to think about the very specific sequence of steps that are required to execute that habit. Here's a trivial example that could be applied to anything. Let's say you want to get into the habit of making yourself or someone else in your household a cup of espresso every morning.

You could actually think through each of those steps: walk into the kitchen, turn on the espresso machine, draw the espresso, etc. You have to walk through each of those steps from start to finish. It turns out that simple mental exercise, done once, can shift people toward a much higher likelihood of performing that habit regularly, not just the first time, but as they continue on into the days and weeks that follow.

The mental exercise of thinking through the sequence of steps required in order to perform a new habit from start to finish can shift the likelihood of being able to perform that habit from unlikely or to moderately likely, to very likely over time.

HOW TO BUILD UP YOUR WILLPOWER AND RESILIENCE?

Huberman suggests you should try getting into a cold shower at 11 o'clock at night. Alternatively, try doing it in the middle of the afternoon. It's quite a different experience because it requires quite a different degree of resilience and leaning into the practice. Your willpower will have to be higher. Huberman suggests late in the day as compared to early in the day, but that will vary, of course, between individuals as well.

How cold should the water be? The answer is uncomfortably cold, to the point where you want to get out, but you can safely stay in. Now you may be wondering whether or not cold showers are as good, better, or worse than cold water immersion up to the neck.

Cold water immersion up to the neck with your feet and hands submerged would be the most effective way to put your willpower to the test. However, the second best thing would be a cold shower that would allow you to experience cold to the point where you would almost want to shiver or start shivering.

By defying ourselves this way, we systematically build up what we call resilience. When we experience a stressor in life, that stress is the consequence of increases in norepinephrine and epinephrine in our brain and body. It's very similar, if not identical, to the kinds of increases that come from deliberate cold exposure.

So, deliberate cold exposure is an opportunity to deliberately stress our bodies. We can learn to maintain mental clarity while our body is in a state of stress. And that can be immensely useful when encountering stress in other parts of life.

WELLBEING

HOW TO LEVERAGE FRUSTRATION?

If you are uncomfortable making errors and you get frustrated easily, Huberman says you can leverage that frustration.

In order to delve deeper into the endeavor, you can set yourself up for a terrific set of plasticity mechanisms to engage. But if you take that frustration and you walk away from the endeavor, you are essentially setting up plasticity to rewire you according to what happens afterwards, which is generally feeling pretty miserable.

So now you can start to appreciate why it is that you continue to drill into a process, to the point of frustration, but then stay with that process for a little bit longer. The most important thing for adult learning, as well as childhood learning, is self-regulation. Well, how do you self-regulate? How do kids self-regulate?

One of the reasons Huberman has gotten excited about public education and teaching neuroscience is that that is a place where knowledge can actually allow oneself to intervene.

WHEN IS STRESS GOOD FOR YOUR IMMUNE SYSTEM?

Dopamine is *the* chemical; it's the molecule from which another molecule called epinephrine is made. Epinephrine has another name, which is adrenaline. Craving and desire are the foundation of stress and fear. how could that possibly be? Well, stress and fear come from adrenaline.

When we are afraid of something, we have one of three responses. We can either remain still or we can retreat. Or we can move forward. All three of those require some increase in our level of activation and the molecule adrenaline. That's what's responsible for getting us moving. It's also responsible for our sense of fear and our paralysis in fear.

But actually, stress is wonderful because it activates our immune system. The stress response recruits the immune organs of the body to release killer T cells.

So, anytime you liberate adrenaline into your bloodstream, you also protect yourself against infection by bacteria and viruses. Think about it in terms of evolution: if we had to gather food and we didn't have it, and we had to then pack up and migrate long distances, you can't afford to get sick.

This is why people who work a lot and then rest usually get sick when they finally stop. Huberman says it's like the post-finals phenomenon in university, or taking care of somebody who's ill. When that stressful period finally stops, you get sick because no stress means that adrenaline gets turned off.

HOW TO REPLENISH YOUR DOPAMINE LEVELS?

When you think, “I'm feeling low, I don't feel good,” then nothing really feels good. Maybe you’re depressed... or maybe you're just saturated in the dopamine circuits -you're now in the painful part.

What do you do? Well, Huberman says that, first of all, you have to stop. Dopamine must be replenished. You need to stop engaging with this behavior, and then your pleasure in it will come back. However, you have to constantly control the hinge. It's not just about being back and forth on the seesaw. You have to make sure the hinge doesn't get stuck in pain or in pleasure.

WHY DOES SUCCESS MAKE THINGS HARDER AND HOW TO DEAL WITH THAT?

If there are people out there who think that the moment they start achieving some success things get easier, they have to face a hard truth right now: things get worse. There are more opportunities and, therefore, your structure gets disrupted more. There's more email, more texts coming in, more amazing possible relationships, more places to eat, and more things to do. Success can actually start to undermine you.

The whole process, if you're not careful, can become a nightmare. This is coming from Huberman, somebody who reached success and knows what it's like firsthand. So how does he cope with his success?

He makes a list every day of simple and enjoyable things he has to do. It literally begins with a dog walk, because the first step is to get some sun. Then he does a 90-minute work block, which means he doesn't use the computer or the internet until much later in the day.

HOW TO USE YOUR BREATHING FOR RELAXATION?

Double inhales followed by an extended exhale are the fastest way to bring the mind and the body into a more relaxed state, according to Huberman. Two inhales through the nose, followed by one to three slow exhales, will reduce your level of autonomic arousal to essentially baseline.

Huberman thinks that this is the best available method of relaxation for anyone that experiences anxiety from time to time -which is everybody.

You can consciously take control over the neurons that control the ratio of carbon dioxide to oxygen in your lungs. Even if you don't remember any of that, it's just two inhales through the nose. What you're trying to do is maximally inflate those little sacks in your lungs, and then exhale slowly through the mouth, this way you're blowing off carbon dioxide.

WHAT'S THE FIRST RULE OF SLEEP?

Huberman says that the first rule of sleep, in general, is to try to get some natural light in your eyes within an hour of waking up. If you wake up before the sun, turn on a bunch of bright lights and then get sunlight in your eyes once it comes out. If there's dense cloud cover, there are still more photons of light energy coming through that cloud cover than there are coming from artificial lights.

So try and get five to 10 minutes without sunglasses outside in the morning. When the sun shines most days, if not every day, it has a significant impact on a variety of factors. First of all, it modulates the timing of what's called the cortisol pulse. Once every 24 hours, you're going to get a boost in cortisol. It's a healthy boost. It sets your temperature rhythm in motion and sets your level of alertness, your level of focus and your mood.

You want that cortisol pulse to happen as early in the day as possible. A cortisol pulse is naturally entrained by these genetic programs to happen once every 24 hours, but light will anchor it to the period where you see bright light.

REVIEWS

This book is a summary of the original book and aims to be of great help for the best analysis and understanding of this.

Thank you for having read this book, we hope that its content has been useful and will serve to deepen your knowledge on the subject. If you really liked the book, we thank you for leaving me a sincere review

The best way for new authors, as is our case, to stand out and get the better positioning of their books is through positive reviews. That way we can continue writing, besides being able to improve the quality day by day.

Thank you very much!

LEGAL DISCLAIMER

This book aims to provide information and entertainment to its readers. Its content is based on sources considered reliable, however, the author cannot confirm or guarantee its accuracy and validity and is not responsible for any error or omission. In no case, the reader must assume the contents of this book as professional advice, nor does it intend to substitute the functions of the experts in the area, therefore, it is a guide whose application should be consulted with the professionals accredited in the area before being used. In the case of protocols or medical treatments described in the contents of this book, the reader must receive qualified professional medical advice before using any of the resources or techniques described in this book.

The reader agrees to accept that by using the information contained in this book, the author is exempt from liability for costs, expenses, damages, and even professional fees that may arise from the application of any detail described in this book. This disclaimer applies even to the direct or indirect application of any information presented, whether due to a breach of contract, grievance, negligence, personal injury, criminal intent or under any other cause of action.

COPYRIGHT

Brain Picking Andrew Huberman: Thoughts And Insights From The Neuroscientist, Professor And Podcaster

By Brain Picking Icons

Author: Brain Picking Icons
Contact: contact@brainpickingicons.com